everyday **STEM**

SCIENCE

ENERGY

Science is all around you!

KINGFISHER
LONDON & NEW YORK

Copyright © Macmillan Publishers International Ltd 2022, 2023
First published 2022
This edition published in 2023 in the United States by Kingfisher
120 Broadway, New York, NY 10271
Kingfisher is an imprint of Macmillan Children's Books, London
All rights reserved.

ISBN 978-0-7534-7779-3 (HC)
978-0-7534-7780-9 (PB)

Distributed in the U.S. and Canada by Macmillan,
120 Broadway, New York, NY 10271

Library of Congress Cataloging-in-Publication data has been applied for.

Author: Dr Shini Somara
Illustrator: Luna Valentine
Series editor: Lizzie Davey
Series design: Jim Green

Kingfisher Books are available for special promotions and premiums.
For details contact:
Special Markets Department, Macmillan
120 Broadway, New York, NY 10271.

For more information please visit:
www.kingfisherbooks.com

Printed in China
2 4 6 8 9 7 5 3 1
1TR/0124/UG/WKT/128MA

EU representative: 1st Floor, The Liffey Trust Centre
117-126 Sheriff Street Upper, Dublin 1 D01 YC43

CONTENTS

4   WHAT IS ENERGY?

6   KINETIC ENERGY

8   POTENTIAL ENERGY

9   CHRISTINA LAMPE-ÖNNERUD

10   POWER AND ENERGY

12   FOSSIL FUELS

14   RENEWABLE ENERGY

16   ENERGY TRANSFER

18   CONVECTION

19   SOPHIE BLANCHARD

20   CONDUCTION

22   RADIATION

24   THE ELECTROMAGNETIC SPECTRUM

26   NUCLEAR ENERGY

28   ELECTRICAL ENERGY

30   ENERGY EFFICIENCY

32   STAYING CONNECTED

34   EARTH'S INTERNAL ENERGY

36   PIEZOELECTRICITY

38   SOLAR ARRAYS

40   RECYCLING RADIO WAVES

TRY THIS AT HOME:

42   MAKE YOUR OWN ELECTROMAGNETS

43   STATIC ELECTRICITY

44   SPLITTING LIGHT

45   CONVECTION CURRENTS

46   GLOSSARY

47   INDEX

48   THE AUTHOR & ILLUSTRATOR

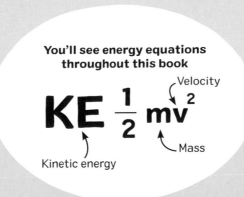

You'll see energy equations throughout this book

$$KE \ \frac{1}{2} \ mv^2$$

Velocity

Mass

Kinetic energy

WHAT IS ENERGY?

Anything that has energy has the ability to do things. This includes everything from really hard work, such as a packed school bus driving uphill, to the not so difficult, such as sleeping. All things that move, change, or even exist have energy, and the more energy they have, the more they can do!

ENERGY IS THE ABILITY TO DO WORK

It takes energy to clean our rooms, for cranes to move heavy objects from one place to another, and for computers to work. Food, gasoline, and electricity are all forms of energy that enable work.

TYPES OF ENERGY

It is not always easy to see where energy comes from, but we can tell that it is there, because of the things that happen when it is used. Anything that changes or moves in some way is using energy. There are many types of energy in the universe, including electricity, chemicals, light, sound, and gravity. Some forms of energy are more useful than others, depending on what you need to use the energy for.

Most of the time energy is converted from one form into another. Energy is really useful for cooking because eating cold pizza and salad isn't always fun!

Wood is a form of fuel, and so is gasoline. Burning wood releases heat. We put gasoline in our cars and scooters to give them energy to move.

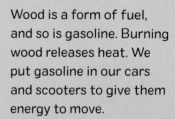

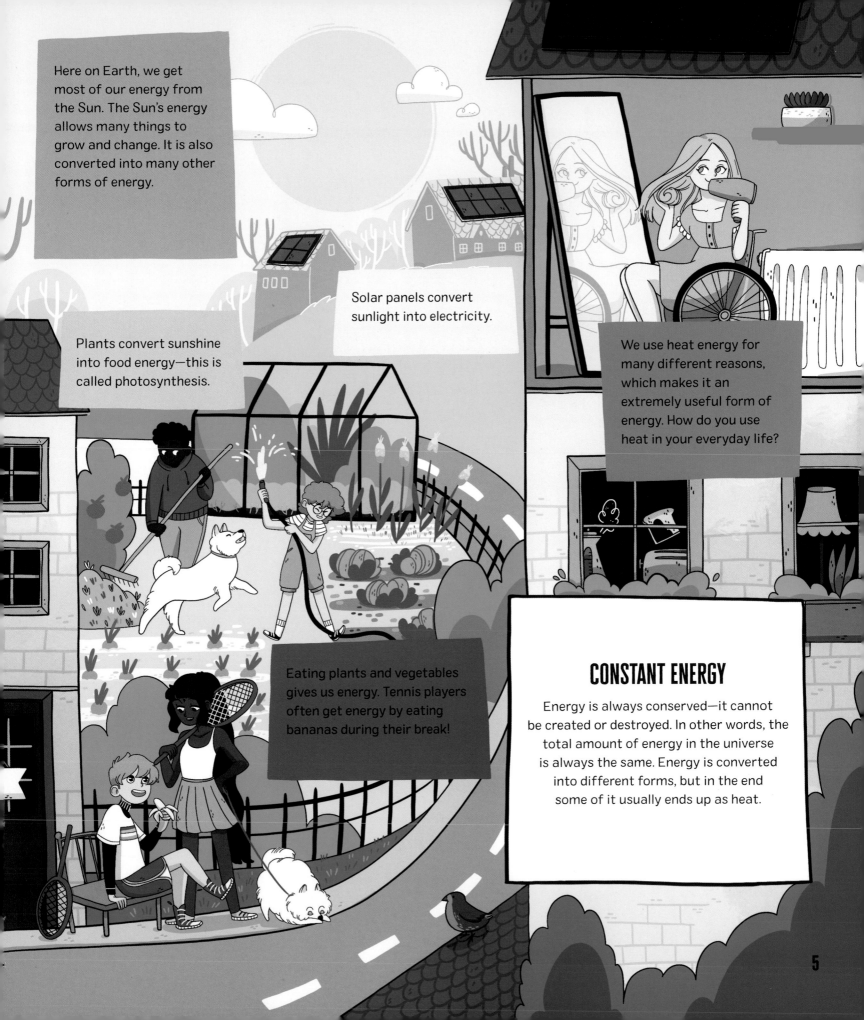

Here on Earth, we get most of our energy from the Sun. The Sun's energy allows many things to grow and change. It is also converted into many other forms of energy.

Solar panels convert sunlight into electricity.

Plants convert sunshine into food energy—this is called photosynthesis.

We use heat energy for many different reasons, which makes it an extremely useful form of energy. How do you use heat in your everyday life?

Eating plants and vegetables gives us energy. Tennis players often get energy by eating bananas during their break!

CONSTANT ENERGY

Energy is always conserved—it cannot be created or destroyed. In other words, the total amount of energy in the universe is always the same. Energy is converted into different forms, but in the end some of it usually ends up as heat.

KINETIC ENERGY

If something moves, it has kinetic energy. The amount of kinetic energy an object has depends on how heavy it is or how fast it is traveling. Different types of energy, such as energy from the Sun, from chemicals, or from gravity can all be converted into kinetic energy.

Kinetic energy is the energy that objects possess due to their motion.

$$KE \quad \frac{1}{2} \, mv^2$$

Kinetic energy

Mass

Velocity

It's hard work pushing a heavy shopping cart. As the cart gets heavier, or if we want to push it faster, we have to give it more kinetic energy.

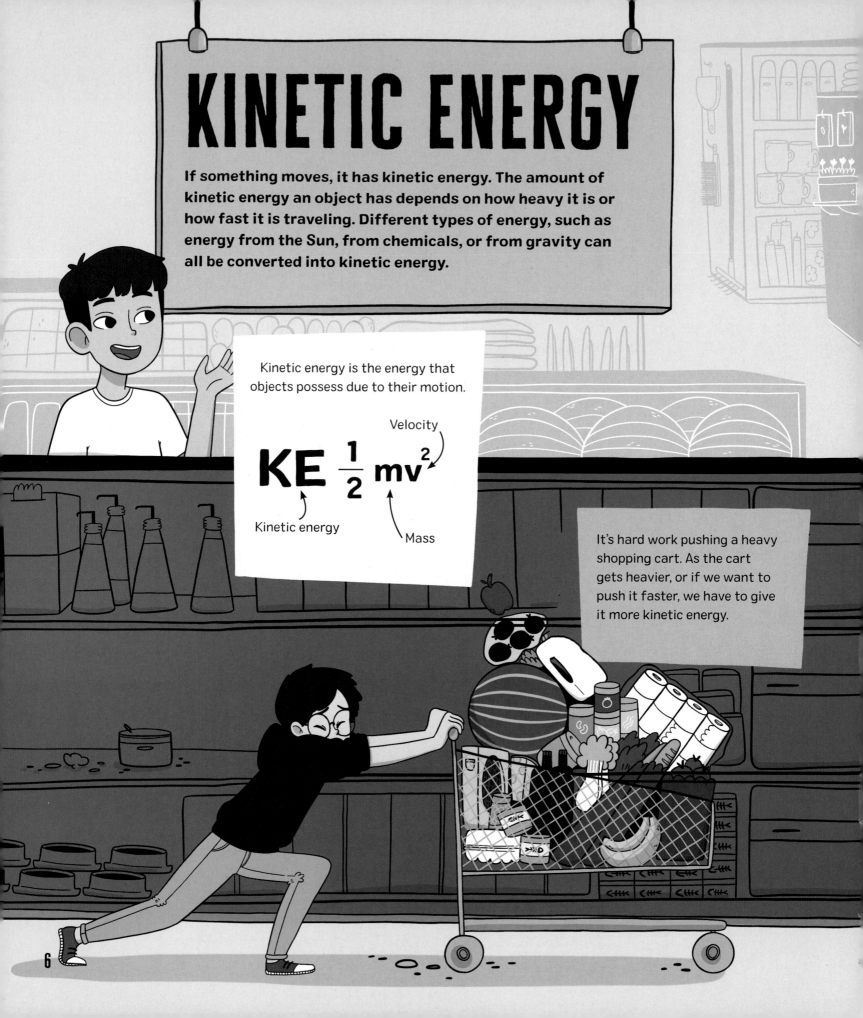

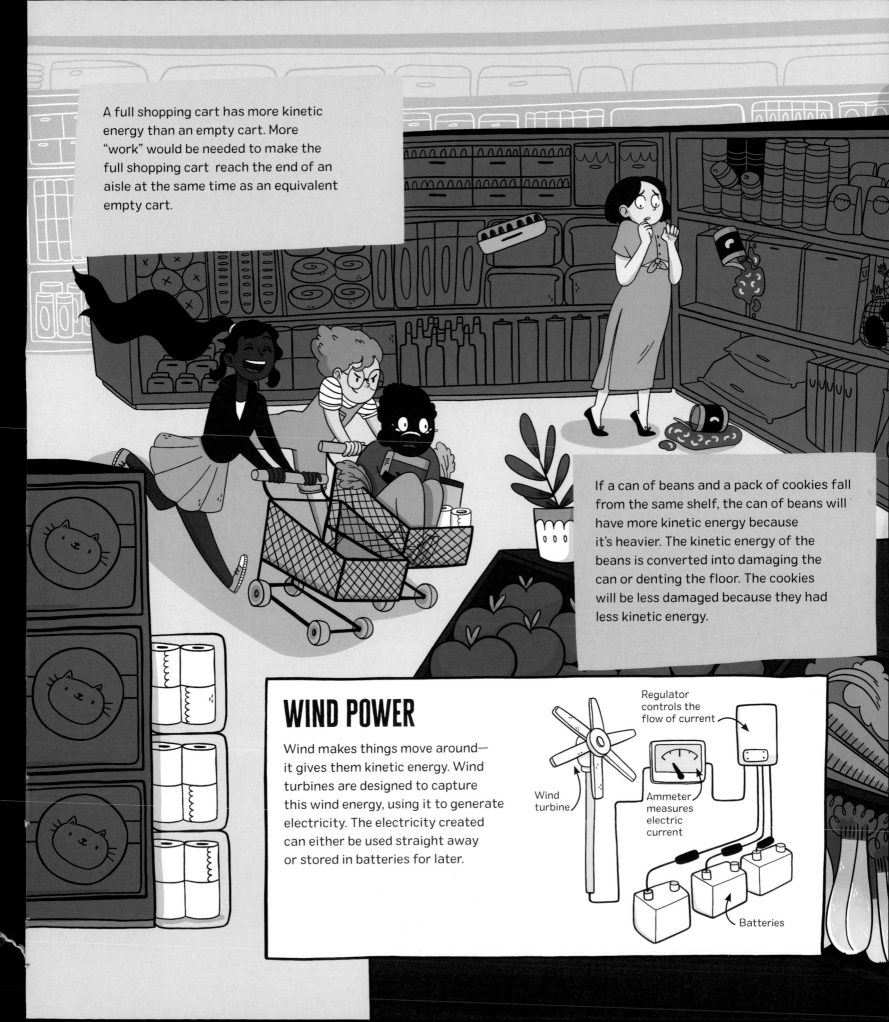

A full shopping cart has more kinetic energy than an empty cart. More "work" would be needed to make the full shopping cart reach the end of an aisle at the same time as an equivalent empty cart.

If a can of beans and a pack of cookies fall from the same shelf, the can of beans will have more kinetic energy because it's heavier. The kinetic energy of the beans is converted into damaging the can or denting the floor. The cookies will be less damaged because they had less kinetic energy.

WIND POWER

Wind makes things move around—it gives them kinetic energy. Wind turbines are designed to capture this wind energy, using it to generate electricity. The electricity created can either be used straight away or stored in batteries for later.

Regulator controls the flow of current

Wind turbine

Ammeter measures electric current

Batteries

POTENTIAL ENERGY

Potential energy is stored energy—energy that has not yet been used but is ready to go. Potential energy can take many forms, including food (chemical), when something is about to fall (gravitational), and coiled springs (mechanical). It's useful because we can save it for when we need it most. Here are a few examples of everyday potential energy.

$$E_p = mgh$$

Potential energy → E_p

Gravity → g

Mass → m

Vertical height → h

ENERGY FROM GRAVITY

Gravity on Earth always pulls objects downward. The farther away an object is from Earth's surface, the more potential energy it will have. The gravitational potential energy of an object increases with height and weight, so heavier objects have more gravitational potential energy. When they are dropped, this quickly converts into kinetic energy.

Batteries contain chemicals that react with each other, releasing their chemical potential energy.

CHEMICAL POTENTIAL ENERGY

Chemical potential energy is energy stored between the atoms and molecules of a substance. Gasoline and wood are useful fuels because they have large quantities of chemical potential energy. When these fuels are burned, their chemical potential energy is released.

ELASTIC POTENTIAL ENERGY

Elastic bands can have elastic potential energy. If enough work is put into stretching the elastic, its stored-up energy can launch an object when the elastic is let go. The elastic potential energy is converted into the kinetic energy of the launched object.

CHRISTINA LAMPE-ÖNNERUD (BORN 1967)

Lithium-ion batteries were first created in the 1970s. They are different from regular batteries, known as alkaline batteries, because they can be recharged. This makes lithium-ion batteries really useful in our phones, computers, and other electronics. Here's the story of how one scientist has worked to improve the batteries we use every day.

Christina Lampe-Önnerud was born in Sweden in 1967. She loved science as a child, studied chemistry, and then began her career as a scientist.

Through her work Lampe-Önnerud became an expert in lithium-ion, or "li-ion" batteries. She started her own company to make them.

Lampe-Önnerud has worked to make li-ion batteries smaller and able to store more energy. To do this, she has had to test many new materials.

Batteries make our devices heavier, so scientists like Lampe-Önnerud are working hard to make batteries smaller, lighter, and more powerful.

Li-ion batteries are used in electric vehicles. Scientists are racing to build batteries that can last longer and take us farther on a single charge.

POWER AND ENERGY

Power is the rate at which work is carried out—it describes how fast energy is being used. Energy is a measure of the amount of work being performed.

To change or move, things need a certain amount of work or energy. If you lift a heavy weight up a flight of stairs, it takes work. Whether you lift that weight slowly or quickly makes no difference to the amount of energy or work needed. The difference between doing work slowly or quickly is power. If you can do the same amount of work in a shorter period of time, that means you have more power available.

$$P = \frac{W}{t}$$

Power, Work, Time

MUSCLE POWER

A big, muscular animal is stronger and able to travel farther and faster than a small baby animal. We can say the adult is more powerful than the baby because it uses more energy per unit of time.

DID YOU KNOW?

Before light bulbs were invented in the early 1800s, people would use candles to see in the dark. Candlelight is not very powerful because a lot of the energy created is wasted as heat.

POWERFUL MACHINES

Powerful machines use lots of energy per unit of time. A high-powered water jet would be perfect for cleaning chewing gum off a sidewalk, but it would be too powerful for cleaning windows.

POWER IN THE RIGHT PLACES

The more powerful a light bulb is, the more energy it uses. High-powered lights can illuminate a stage or football field, while less powerful lights are useful in our homes. Light bulbs with a higher power rating use more electricity.

HOW A STEAM ENGINE WORKS

Steam engines convert heat energy from steam into kinetic (movement) energy, which means they can be used to power all kinds of things. In 1769, James Watt came up with an improvement to earlier steam engines that made them much more powerful and therefore more useful. Watt's steam engine was so important that our unit of power is named after him—we measure power in watts.

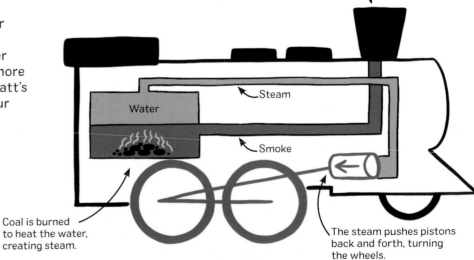

Water

Steam

Smoke

Coal is burned to heat the water, creating steam.

The steam pushes pistons back and forth, turning the wheels.

FOSSIL FUELS

Almost all energy on Earth comes from the Sun—it is the Sun's energy that allows plants and animals to live. When these living things die, they break down, becoming part of the Earth again. Over millions of years this process has created thick layers of decay, which we call fossil fuels. Fossil fuels contain huge amounts of chemical potential energy. There are three types: coal, oil, and natural gas. We use them to cook, to heat homes, and to generate electricity. Earth has a limited quantity of fossil fuels— eventually we will use them all up.

HOW COAL IS FORMED

Millions of years ago, Earth was covered in forests and animals such as the dinosaurs.

When the forest plants and animals died and their remains were left behind.

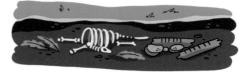

The remains were covered over and compressed.

Over time, heat and pressure turned the remains plants into coal.

REACHING FOSSIL FUELS

Coal is a solid fuel that has to be dug out of the ground. Oil and natural gas are mostly found in patches under the seabed. Engineers use enormous engineering equipment to reach down into Earth to access fossil fuels and bring them up to the surface so that we can use them.

Coal miners work in tunnels underground. They dig out coal from deep beneath Earth's surface.

If coal is near the surface, the rock above it can be blasted away, making the coal easier to reach.

Oil rigs drill down into the seabed, then pump oil and natural gas up to the rig. The fuels are then shipped across to land.

THE GREENHOUSE EFFECT

Greenhouses are designed to keep the space inside them warm by trapping heat from the Sun. Earth's atmosphere traps the Sun's heat around our planet in a similar way. An increasing greenhouse effect means that temperatures on Earth are rising. Snow and ice are melting and sea levels are rising. Burning fossil fuels releases harmful gases into the atmosphere, trapping even more heat. Scientists and engineers are trying to find cleaner and kinder sources of energy that don't harm our precious planet.

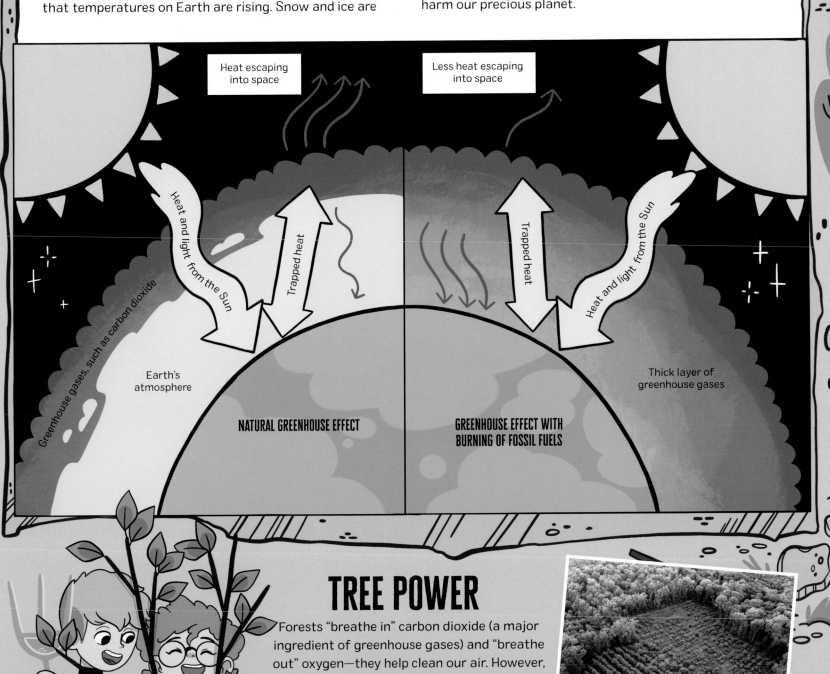

Heat escaping into space

Less heat escaping into space

Heat and light from the Sun

Trapped heat

Greenhouse gases, such as carbon dioxide

Earth's atmosphere

NATURAL GREENHOUSE EFFECT

Trapped heat

Heat and light from the Sun

Thick layer of greenhouse gases

GREENHOUSE EFFECT WITH BURNING OF FOSSIL FUELS

TREE POWER

Forests "breathe in" carbon dioxide (a major ingredient of greenhouse gases) and "breathe out" oxygen—they help clean our air. However, trees get chopped down because wood is so useful as a fuel and as a material. To help our planet, we need to make sure we plant more trees to replace those we cut down.

RENEWABLE ENERGY

Renewable energy is sustainable—it is always replaced and will never run out. There will always be wind, waves, and flowing water, and we can convert their kinetic energy into electricity. Renewable energy is generated and used in many ways—here are some everyday examples.

SAILBOATS

The sails on sailboats harness the power of the wind to move them along. Sailors have been using this clean energy since long before we invented big powerful engines to move us across the ocean.

SOLAR PANELS

Solar cells convert solar energy from sunlight into electricity. They even work on cloudy days. Some people put solar panels on their roofs to power their homes and heat their water.

WIND TURBINES

The kinetic energy in wind spins wind turbine blades around, generating electricity that can power many homes. In some places you might see huge wind turbines in the distance as you drive along a highway.

SOLAR PANELS IN SPACE

We don't just use solar panels on Earth! The International Space Station gets most of its power from solar cells that are spread out across eight solar array wings.

DID YOU KNOW?

The Sun should keep providing us with light and heat for the next 5 billion years. Covering just 1 percent of the Sahara desert in solar panels would generate enough electricity to power the entire world.

WATER POWER

Flowing water has been used to power watermills for thousands of years. Giant hydroelectric dams now harness the power of water in the same way. The potential energy of the water stored at the top of the dam is converted into kinetic energy as the water falls.

MARIA TELKES (1900–1995)

Maria Telkes studied physical chemistry at the University of Budapest in Hungary. She created the first solar-powered heating system for the home in the late 1940s. Telkes went on to create many other solar-powered devices, including the world's first solar electric house in 1980. Her work with solar power earned her the nickname "Sun Queen."

ENERGY TRANSFER

Energy transfer takes place when energy moves from one thing to another. When we kick a soccer ball, kinetic energy in our moving foot is transferred to move the ball. In our homes, electrical energy is transferred into kinetic energy in our washing machines, light energy in our light bulbs, and sound energy in our music systems. In most energy transfers, heat, also known as thermal energy, is created too.

THERMAL ENERGY

Sometimes converting one form of energy into thermal energy is exactly what is needed. For example, a coffee maker converts electrical energy into thermal energy to heat water. However, sometimes thermal energy is created where it is not wanted. For example, if the battery in your phone heats up, it may be faulty.

SOLID
The particles in frozen water have very little kinetic energy—they hardly move.

Water freezes at 32° on the Fahrenheit scale (0° Celsius).

LIQUID
When ice melts, it takes thermal energy from its surroundings. The particles melt because their kinetic energy increases.

GAS
The particles in steam have so much kinetic energy that they are able to turn turbines and generate electricity.

When water boils, it has a high temperature. The particles in boiling water are moving a lot—they have lots of kinetic energy. Water boils at 212°F (100°C).

As air warms up, it gains kinetic energy and rises.

As air cools, it loses kinetic energy and sinks down.

WHAT IS TEMPERATURE?

All things are made up of particles. Temperature indicates how much kinetic energy these particles have—it is a measure of how warm or cold something is. We use three main scales to measure temperature.

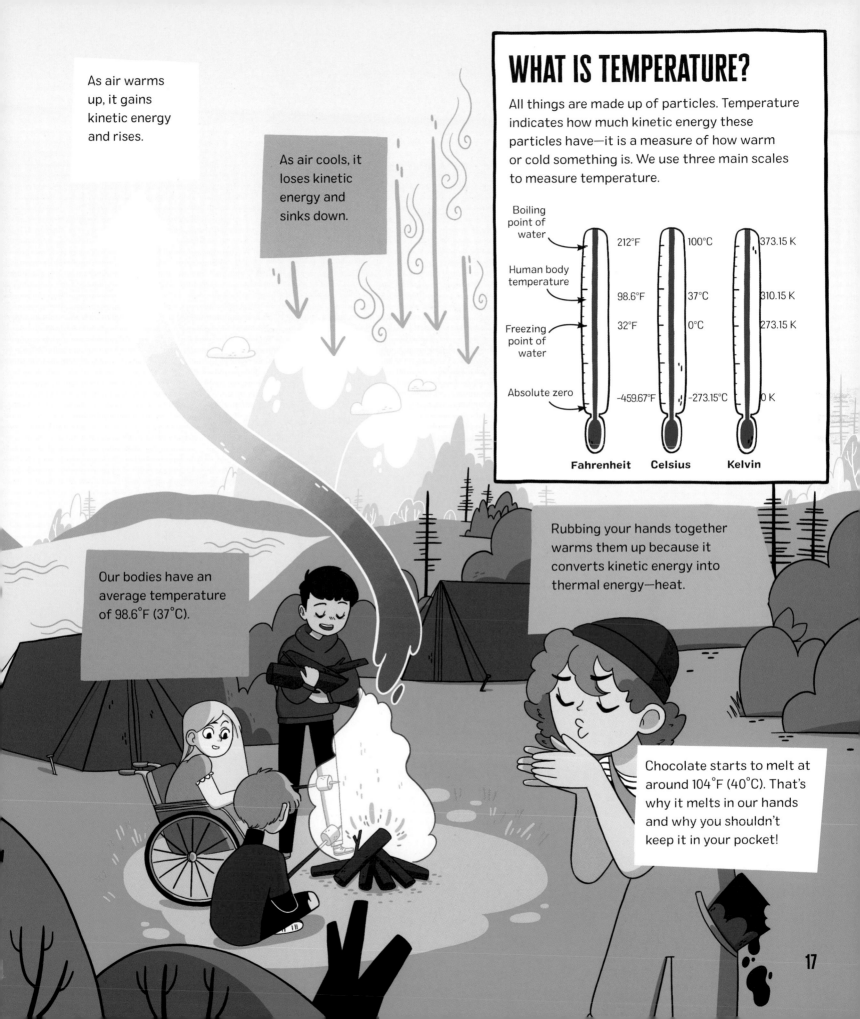

Boiling point of water — 212°F — 100°C — 373.15 K

Human body temperature — 98.6°F — 37°C — 310.15 K

Freezing point of water — 32°F — 0°C — 273.15 K

Absolute zero — -459.67°F — -273.15°C — 0 K

Fahrenheit   **Celsius**   **Kelvin**

Our bodies have an average temperature of 98.6°F (37°C).

Rubbing your hands together warms them up because it converts kinetic energy into thermal energy—heat.

Chocolate starts to melt at around 104°F (40°C). That's why it melts in our hands and why you shouldn't keep it in your pocket!

CONVECTION

Warm air has more kinetic energy than cold air—it likes to rise, expand, and travel. It tends to move toward cooler places. Cool air has less kinetic energy, so it prefers to sink. The movement of heat according to these rules is called convection.

WIND

Differences in temperature can make air move. On a big scale, masses of hot air next to cold air can create wind. The larger the temperature difference, the more kinetic energy the wind will have. Tornadoes have more power than hurricanes, and hurricanes have more power than a light breeze.

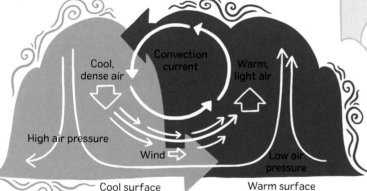

Convection current

Cool, dense air

Warm, light air

High air pressure

Wind

Low air pressure

Cool surface

Warm surface

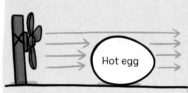

Hot egg

Natural convection

Hot egg

Forced convection

FORCED CONVECTION

We can direct convection currents using fans, hair dryers, hand dryers, or bicycle pumps. These devices can force air to travel in a certain direction. In the example above, a fan is used to push the warm air in a certain direction.

TURBULENCE

Have you ever been shaken around by turbulence during an airplane flight? If so, you've felt the effect of giant convection currents for yourself.

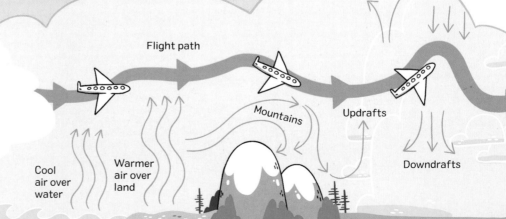

Flight path

Mountains

Updrafts

Downdrafts

Cool air over water

Warmer air over land

SOPHIE BLANCHARD (1778–1819)

Sophie Blanchard was born in 1778.

She became a pioneering French aeronaut. Over her lifetime Blanchard made more than 60 ascents in a hot-air balloon.

Blanchard was the first woman to pilot her own hot-air balloon and the first to make a career from ballooning. Her spectacular solo flights mesmerized crowds.

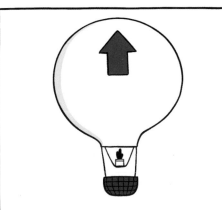

Hot-air balloons work using the principle of convection. Gas burners blow hot air into the balloon, making it rise.

Sadly, in 1819 Blanchard became the first woman to be killed in an aviation accident. Her fatal accident was probably caused by the gas burners setting the balloon on fire.

CONDUCTION

If two things that are different temperatures touch, the faster-moving atoms in the hotter thing will transfer kinetic energy to the slower-moving atoms in the colder thing. As a result, the slower-moving atoms in the colder substance speed up, making it heat up, and the faster-moving atoms in the hotter thing slow down, making it cool. This process is called conduction. It happens when thermal energy (heat) or electricity is transferred between objects that are touching.

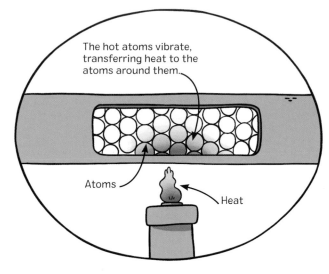

The hot atoms vibrate, transferring heat to the atoms around them.

Atoms

Heat

HUMANS

Our bodies are about 60 percent water, which means the human body is a good conductor of electricity. So you should avoid standing outside near a puddle in a thunderstorm!

RUBBER

Rubber is a terrible conductor of thermal and electrical energy. It is used to make place mats for hot cups and plates. The rubber stops the heat from traveling from the cup or plate into the table.

WATER

Water is good at conducting electricity, which is why you should be very careful with electrical outlets in a bathroom. Water near an outlet could be deadly. Never put an electrical item near water.

ELECTRICAL WIRES

A conductor is a material that electricity or heat can flow through. Metals make great electrical conductors, which is why most electrical wires are metal. Plastics are terrible electrical conductors, which is why metal wires are covered by plastic coatings. The plastic allows us to touch the coated wire without getting an electric shock.

Metal wire

Plastic coating

CERAMICS

Ceramics are not good conductors at all. We use them to make mugs and plates, which we can touch without burning our hands.

METALS

Most metals are great conductors of thermal and electrical energy. Cooking pots are usually made from metal because the heat from the stove can conduct through the metal easily, heating up the food inside.

RADIATION

Thermal radiation is invisible waves of heat. These invisible waves are emitted by everything on Earth that is warmer than absolute zero on the Kelvin scale. The warmer something is, the more thermal radiation it can emit. It is thermal radiation that allows us to warm up in front of a fire, and thermal radiation that is emitted when an old-fashioned light bulb or radiator becomes hot.

INFRARED WAVES

Thermal radiation cannot be seen with the human eye because it is just outside our visible spectrum. However, infrared cameras can detect thermal radiation. They turn the heat they detect into colors we can see.

NORMAL VIEW
The radiator emits heat, but we are unable to see how hot it is.

INFRARED CAMERA
An infrared camera uses color to show heat. The red areas are the hottest.

Convection
When hot particles in a liquid or gas take the place of colder particles.

Conduction
When heat energy travels along something, from a hot part to a colder part

Radiation
Heat transfer in waves, with no particles involved

MOVING THROUGH NOTHING

Heat is transferred in three ways: convection, conduction, and radiation. Heat transfer by radiation doesn't need to travel through any solid, liquid, or gas. This is how the Sun's rays reach Earth—solar radiation travels superfast, through the nothingness of space.

REFLECTING HEAT

Dark, dull surfaces give off more thermal radiation than bright, shiny surfaces. Surfaces that give off a lot of thermal radiation also absorb a lot of thermal radiation. This is why it is always best to wear light colors in the summer—they will not absorb as much heat as darker colors. People also put reflectors over their cars' windscreens to keep the inside of the car as cool as possible.

ABSOLUTE ZERO

There is a temperature where particles in substances have no kinetic energy at all. The particles are completely still and emit no thermal radiation. This temperature is called absolute zero. It measures –459.67°F on the Fahrenheit scale (–273.15°C). Here are two scientists who made huge contributions to our understanding of absolute zero.

Guillaume Amontons (1663–1705) was a French inventor who never went to college. In 1702 he managed to figure out the concept of absolute zero all on his own. He did many experiments on air temperature and estimated that absolute zero must be around –400°F (–240°C). Amontons's estimate was only a few degrees off the actual value, which wasn't discovered until almost 150 years later!

William Thomson (1824–1907) was a Scottish-Irish physicist better known as Lord Kelvin. In 1848 he developed Amontons's work and came up with an "absolute" temperature scale that would apply to all substances, not just air. He named his scale after himself and set absolute zero as 0 kelvin. The Kelvin scale allows us to easily compare extremely low temperatures.

THE ELECTROMAGNETIC SPECTRUM

Have you seen waves in the sea? The waves are continually moving. Heat, light, and energy travel in waves too, though most of them are invisible to us. How much energy these waves have depends on their wavelength.

WAVELENGTH

A wavelength is the distance from peak to peak between waves. Short wavelengths have more energy, and longer wavelengths have less energy.

FREQUENCY

Frequency is the number of wavelengths per unit time. It is measured in Hertz.

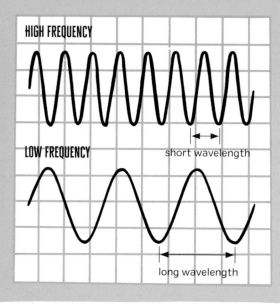

HIGH FREQUENCY

LOW FREQUENCY

short wavelength

long wavelength

SOUND

Sound also travels in waves. However, it has longer wavelengths than electromagnetic radiation and needs something to travel through. Sound travels much more slowly than light, which is why you see an airplane before you hear it and why the sound of thunder follows behind a flash of lightning.

Longer wavelengths

The electromagnetic radiation spectrum shows us a variety of wavelengths in size order.

RADIO WAVES are used to send sounds and messages over long distances.

MICROWAVES have enough kinetic energy in their wavelengths to reheat yesterday's leftovers! In between radio waves and microwaves is Wi-Fi—something most of us cannot live without.

INFRARED is invisible to us, but we can feel it as heat.

SPLITTING LIGHT

Prisms are a great way to see all the colors that make up nautral light. As the light shines through the prism, it bends, splitting the light into all of its different colors.

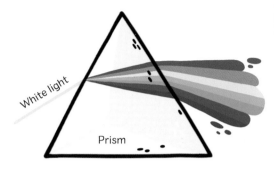

White light

Prism

RAINBOWS

When there is rain and sunshine, the raindrops act like tiny prisms, splitting white light into all its different wavelengths and colors.

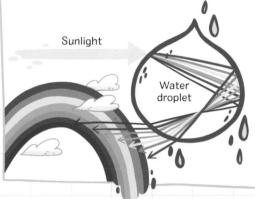

Sunlight

Water droplet

MARIE CURIE (1867-1934)

Marie Curie worked with radioactive materials that emit radiation with very short wavelengths. She made a huge contribution to finding treatments for cancer, using radiation to destroy unhealthy cells in the body.

During the World War I, Curie worked to develop small, mobile X-ray units that could be used to diagnose injuries and locate bone fractures, bullets, and shrapnel in the bodies of the wounded.

Modern X-ray machines allow doctors to examine moving images of the body, such as the pumping action of the heart. These machines are based on the technology that was developed by Marie Curie.

Shorter wavelengths →

VISIBLE LIGHT is the only form of electromagnetic radiation we can see. Different wavelengths of light have different colors—red is the longest and violet the shortest.

ULTRAVIOLET radiation has a shorter wavelength than the color violet. Ultraviolet light makes some substances glow in the dark.

X-RAYS have enough kinetic energy that they can travel through our skin but not our bones. They are useful for looking inside our bodies.

GAMMA RAYS are used to zap unhealthy cells out of our bodies. We have to be careful with very short wavelength electromagnetic radiation. The shorter the wavelength, the more energy the radiation has and the more dangerous it is to our health.

NUCLEAR ENERGY

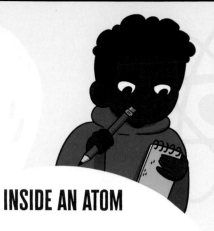

Nuclear energy is a very powerful type of energy. It is released when the nucleus of an atom changes. An atom is the smallest unit of matter and is made up of protons, neutrons, and electrons. When their arrangement is changed, heat energy is released. There are two ways of changing the nucleus of an atom in order to release its huge potential energy: nuclear fission and nuclear fusion. The energy released is used to heat water into steam. This steam then turns turbines, which can generate electricity to power our homes, schools, offices, and factories.

INSIDE AN ATOM

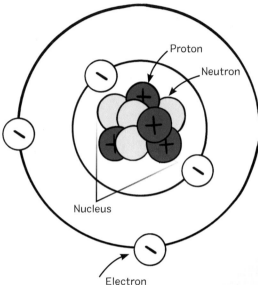

Proton

Neutron

Nucleus

Electron

NUCLEAR FISSION

Nuclear fission is a process in which atoms are split apart, releasing huge amounts of energy. We use fission to generate nuclear power, by splitting uranium atoms. Fission creates huge amounts of power without creating greenhouse gas emissions. However, there are major downsides—the ingredients involved in the reaction are very radioactive. Radioactive materials emit very short wavelength, high energy radiation that is extremely dangerous for our health and the health of our environment.

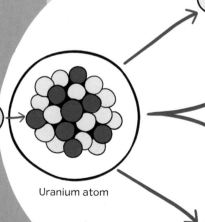

Uranium atom

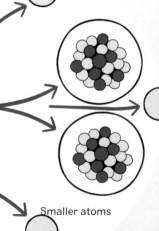

Smaller atoms

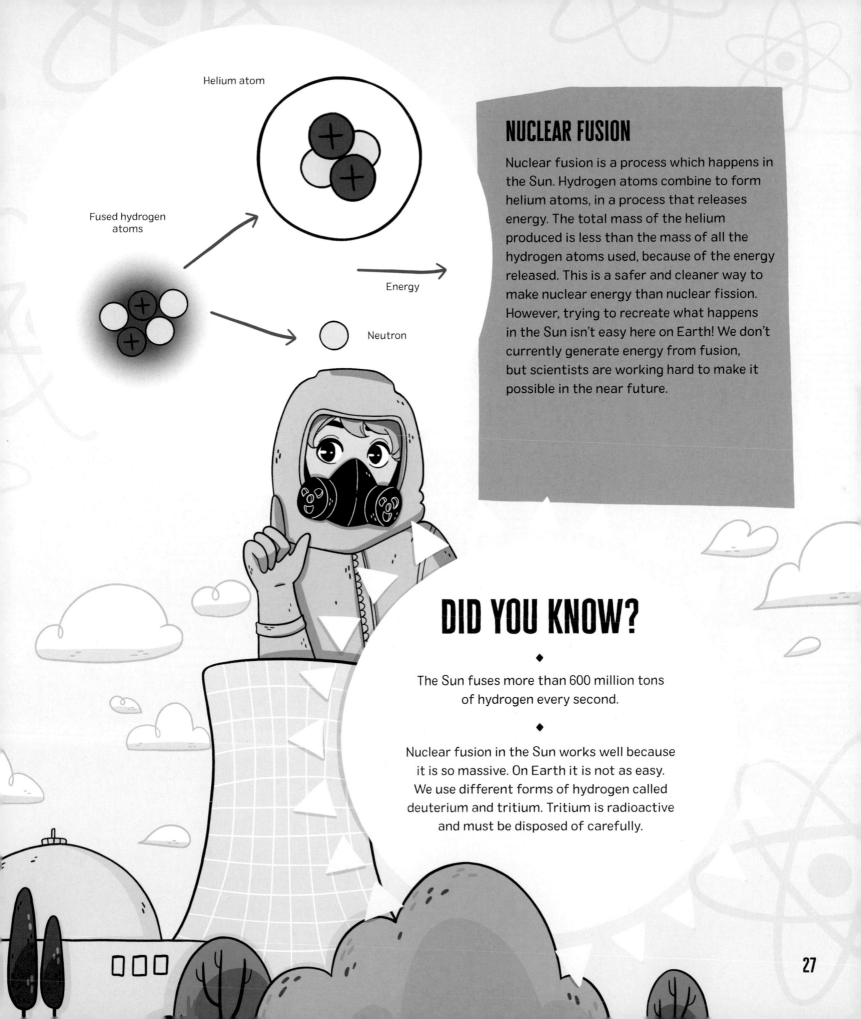

Helium atom

Fused hydrogen atoms

Energy

Neutron

NUCLEAR FUSION

Nuclear fusion is a process which happens in the Sun. Hydrogen atoms combine to form helium atoms, in a process that releases energy. The total mass of the helium produced is less than the mass of all the hydrogen atoms used, because of the energy released. This is a safer and cleaner way to make nuclear energy than nuclear fission. However, trying to recreate what happens in the Sun isn't easy here on Earth! We don't currently generate energy from fusion, but scientists are working hard to make it possible in the near future.

DID YOU KNOW?

◆

The Sun fuses more than 600 million tons of hydrogen every second.

◆

Nuclear fusion in the Sun works well because it is so massive. On Earth it is not as easy. We use different forms of hydrogen called deuterium and tritium. Tritium is radioactive and must be disposed of carefully.

ELECTRICAL ENERGY

Electrical energy is a form of kinetic or moving energy, because it involves electrons flowing around. Electrical energy is used in circuits, but it is also found in nature—a bolt of lightning occurs when a large number of electrons flow between the air and the ground. It has taken us more than 100 years to understand how to produce and control electrical energy. Today electrical outlets are found all over our homes, schools, offices, and everywhere. Our lives would be very different without electricity.

CIRCUITS

For an electric current to happen, there must be a circuit. In a circuit, electricity flows along a loop of metal wire, which links together electrical components such as batteries, switches, and light bulbs. If there is a break in the circuit, electricity cannot flow around it. Switches create a deliberate break in a circuit so that things can be turned off and on.

STATIC ELECTRICITY

Remember those tiny particles called electrons that orbit around the edges of atoms? Each electron has a small negative charge. If two objects rub against each other, electrons can move between them, creating an electric charge on the surface of one object. This is called static electricity. Some materials are more likely to become statically charged than others. If you rub a balloon against your sweater, you create static electricity.

EDITH CLARKE (1883–1959)

In 1918, Edith Clarke became the first woman to earn an electrical engineering degree from the Massachusetts Institute of Technology. She worked at General Electric from 1919 until 1945, becoming an electrical engineer after just two years of employment, which was an impressive achievement for a woman at the time. In 1921 she received her first patent, for the Clarke Calculator—a device that was used to solve problems in delivering electricity along power lines. Clarke went on to teach electrical engineering at the University of Texas, making her the first female professor of electrical engineering in the United States.

Electricity flows along the wire and into the phone's battery.

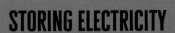

STORING ELECTRICITY

When electricity is stored in one place, such as in a battery, it has potential energy—the potential to be used in the future. When you turn your phone on, it uses the energy stored in its battery. To charge the battery, we plug the phone into an electrical outlet and electrons flow into the battery, to be stored there again.

DID YOU KNOW?

Electric power poles and transmission towers are found all over the country and are connected by power lines. Sometimes these power lines carry colored balls known as visibility marker balls. They are there to make sure that the power lines can be seen by aircraft flying overhead.

ENERGY EFFICIENCY

In an ideal world, all the energy you put in to something would do useful work. In reality, that is not often the case. Some of the energy that we put into a system is wasted, usually as heat. Engineers and scientists are always looking for ways to waste less energy by making systems more efficient.

WASTED ENERGY

Efficiency is about putting the minimum amount of energy in, in order to get the maximum amount of work out. If you were really efficient with your homework, you would spend hardly any time on it and get amazing grades! It's the same with energy.

75% HEAT ENERGY (WASTE)

100% PRIMARY FUEL (FOOD)

25% KINETIC ENERGY (MOVEMENT)

EFFICIENCY AT HOME

Huge amounts of energy is needed to power our homes; we measure it in kilowatt hours (kWh). Using 1 kWh, you could boil a kettle 10 times or watch TV for 6 hours. An average household uses 3,730 kWh per year! It's important for our planet that we try not to waste energy, because generating electricity usually requires burning fossil fuels, which damages our environment. There are many things we can do at home to help us use energy more efficiently.

STANDBY MODE

Standby mode is when devices are plugged in but not being used. Televisions, radios, and washing machines all consume a small amount of energy when in standby mode. This is not an efficient use of electrical energy. But don't forget to ask permission before you unplug these devices!

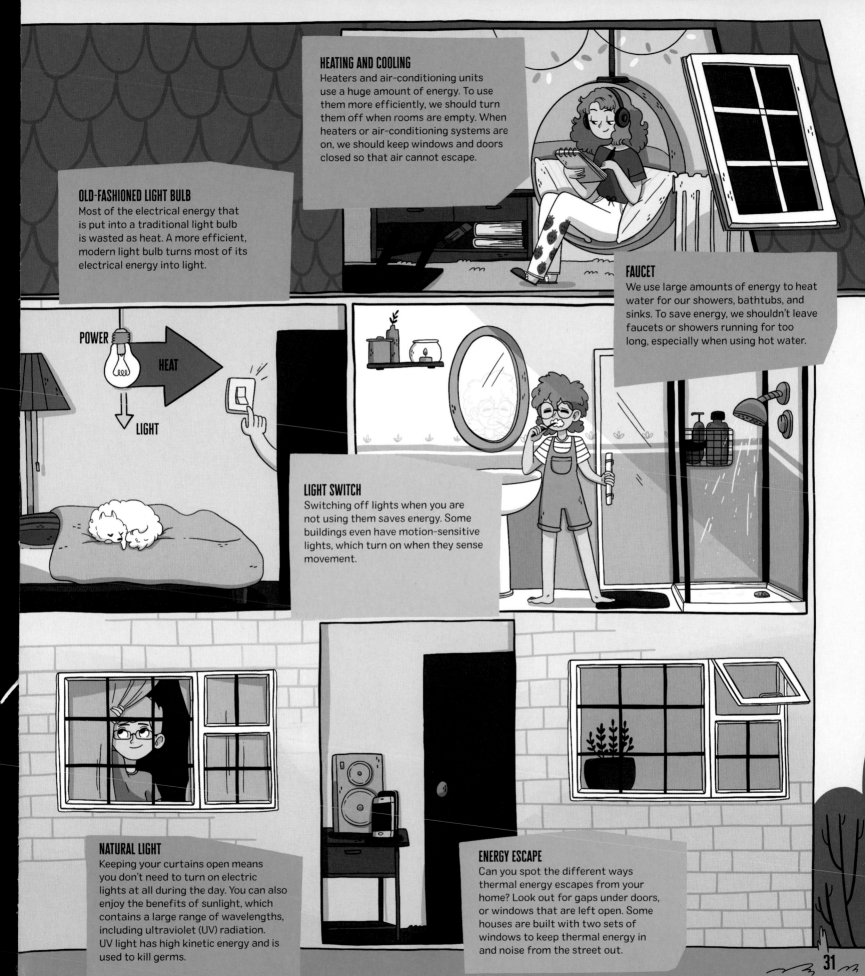

HEATING AND COOLING

Heaters and air-conditioning units use a huge amount of energy. To use them more efficiently, we should turn them off when rooms are empty. When heaters or air-conditioning systems are on, we should keep windows and doors closed so that air cannot escape.

OLD-FASHIONED LIGHT BULB

Most of the electrical energy that is put into a traditional light bulb is wasted as heat. A more efficient, modern light bulb turns most of its electrical energy into light.

POWER

HEAT

LIGHT

FAUCET

We use large amounts of energy to heat water for our showers, bathtubs, and sinks. To save energy, we shouldn't leave faucets or showers running for too long, especially when using hot water.

LIGHT SWITCH

Switching off lights when you are not using them saves energy. Some buildings even have motion-sensitive lights, which turn on when they sense movement.

NATURAL LIGHT

Keeping your curtains open means you don't need to turn on electric lights at all during the day. You can also enjoy the benefits of sunlight, which contains a large range of wavelengths, including ultraviolet (UV) radiation. UV light has high kinetic energy and is used to kill germs.

ENERGY ESCAPE

Can you spot the different ways thermal energy escapes from your home? Look out for gaps under doors, or windows that are left open. Some houses are built with two sets of windows to keep thermal energy in and noise from the street out.

STAYING CONNECTED

We are able to see and hear people all around the world whenever we want! This is all thanks to electromagnetic energy. Converting sound energy, light energy, and electrical energy into electromagnetic energy allows us to communicate. The most useful thing about electromagnetic energy is that it can travel for long distances through empty space. Telephones, televisions, radios, and Wi-Fi all use electromagnetic energy to help us to stay connected.

REMEMBER!

Electromagnetic energy is different from sound energy. Sound is not part of the electromagnetic spectrum because it must travel through something, such as air or water.

The first big step in telecommunication was the telegraph in the 1830s. It could send pulses of electrical energy along a metal wire. By 1866 thick cables had been laid down under the Atlantic Ocean, and electrical pulses could be sent between North America and Europe.

Longer wavelength radio waves are used to direct radio-controlled cars.

By 1907 sound waves and electric pulses could be converted into a range of long electromagnetic wavelengths called radio waves. All radio wavelengths can travel through air. This meant that wires and cables could be replaced with transmission towers.

	MARITIME RADIO, NAVIGATION	MARITIME RADIO, NAVIGATION	AM RADIO, AVIATION RADIO, NAVIGATION	SHORTWAVE RADIO
FREQUENCY	30 kHz	300 kHz		3 MHz
WAVELENGTH	10 km	1 km		100 m

FIBER OPTICS

Another way of sending and receiving signals is fiber optics, which use light sent down a glass cable. Electromagnetic waves always travel in a straight direction, so the light bounces in straight lines along the cable walls. Fiber optic cables provide us with TV, radio, telephone calls, and Internet data.

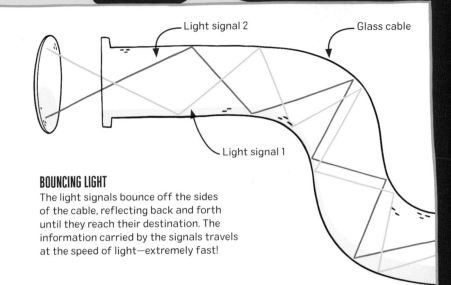

Light signal 2 · Glass cable · Light signal 1

BOUNCING LIGHT

The light signals bounce off the sides of the cable, reflecting back and forth until they reach their destination. The information carried by the signals travels at the speed of light—extremely fast!

By the 1930s, television broadcasts were possible, because physicists had figured out how to convert sounds, light, and electrical pulses into radio waves and beam them from transmission towers.

Shorter wavelength radio waves are used in GPS and radar systems for monitoring traffic and the weather. The more energy the radio waves have, the more powerful they are.

"Radar" stands for Radio Detecting And Ranging. Radar is used for traffic control and weather monitoring and by the military. Longer wavelength radio waves are sent out and scatter when they hit objects, including rain, speeding cars, airplanes, and ships.

Satellite TV uses a mixture of radio waves and microwaves. Microwaves have shorter wavelengths and more kinetic energy, so they can carry more information. TV providers send their microwaves to a satellite, and the satellite sends the signals back to Earth.

VHF TELEVISION, FM RADIO	UHF TELEVISION, CELL PHONES, GPS, WI-FI, 4G, RADAR	SATELLITE COMMUNICATIONS	RADIO ASTRONOMY, SATELLITE COMMUNICATIONS
300MHz	3 GHz	30 GHz	300 GHz
1 m	10 cm	1 cm	1 mm

EARTH'S INTERNAL ENERGY

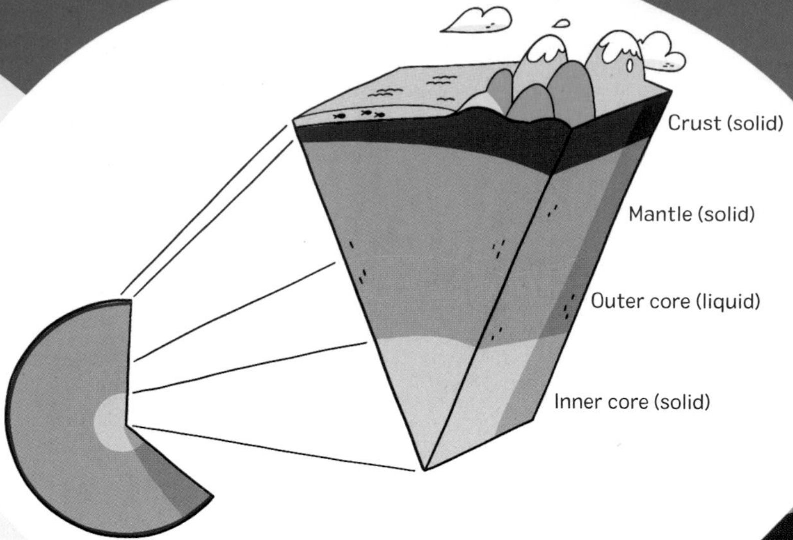

Crust (solid)

Mantle (solid)

Outer core (liquid)

Inner core (solid)

When Earth formed 4.5 billion years ago, the whole planet was liquid. Since then it has been cooling down and solidifying. If we were to look at a slice of Earth, we would see that it has a solid iron inner core but that its outer core is formed from liquid iron. The crust of Earth, which is the part we live on, is the thinnest layer of all. Earth still contains a huge amount of heat, which makes it a major source of thermal energy. We call this geothermal energy.

Fumaroles are openings in Earth's surface that send out volcanic gases and steam.

GEOTHERMAL FEATURES

We can see evidence of the heat inside Earth from its surface—for example, when volcanoes erupt, sending out bright red lava. Lava is rock that is so hot it has become liquid. Geysers, fumaroles, and hot springs also show us where Earth's internal heat is escaping through its crust.

Geysers are hot springs that send jets of water into the sky.

Volcanic eruption

ICELAND

Iceland is an active volcanic area, with geothermal energy close to Earth's surface. Icelanders are able to pump hot water straight from the ground. They use fewer fossil fuels than other parts of the world, thanks to Iceland's geothermal energy.

GEOTHERMAL POWER PLANT

Geothermal energy can be used to generate electricity. The heat is used to turn water into steam, which then turns turbines to generate electricity. In some parts of the world where geothermal energy is not so easy to access, we have to drill deep into Earth to reach it.

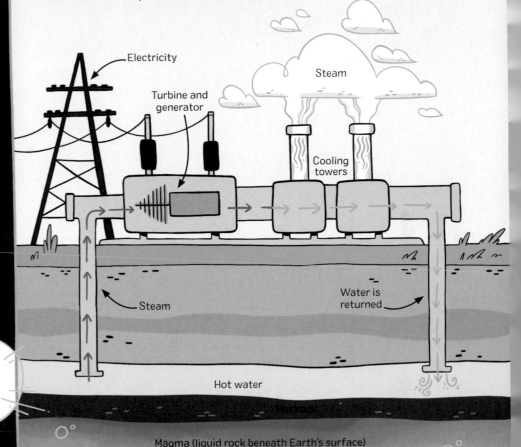

Electricity

Turbine and generator

Steam

Cooling towers

Steam

Water is returned

Hot water

Hot rock

Magma (liquid rock beneath Earth's surface)

DID YOU KNOW?

Geothermal energy from natural pools and hot springs has long been used for cooking, bathing, and warmth. It was used for cooking as early as 10,000 years ago, and in ancient times the Greeks and Romans used baths heated by hot springs. Today geothermally-generated electricity can be used for pretty much anything!

FUTURE EARTH

Scientists predict that when Earth's core cools completely, Earth might become like Mars, with a very thin atmosphere and no more volcanic eruptions or earthquakes. It will be difficult for life to survive. Don't worry, though—we won't have to think about this possibility for several billion years!

PIEZOELECTRICITY

Certain materials can generate an electric charge when they are squeezed or pushed—this is called a piezoelectric effect. The word "piezoelectric" originates from the Greek word "piezein," which means to squeeze or press. There are many things in our daily life which use piezoelectricity, such as battery-powered watches, speakers, alarms, microphones, butane lighters, and the touch screen on your phone. But how do they work?

1. DISORDERLY CRYSTALS

Piezoelectric crystals are electrically neutral—their electric charges are balanced. However, their atomic structure is very disorderly, which is unusual for a crystal.

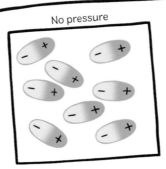
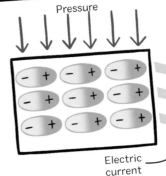

No pressure

Pressure

Electric current created

2. SQUEEZE OR STRETCH

Squeezing or stretching a piezoelectric crystal changes its structure, pushing the atoms around and upsetting the balance of positive and negative charges. This imbalance creates an electrical charge. The crystal becomes a kind of tiny battery, with a positive charge on one face and a negative charge on the other. If we connect the two faces together to make a circuit, then an electric current will flow between them.

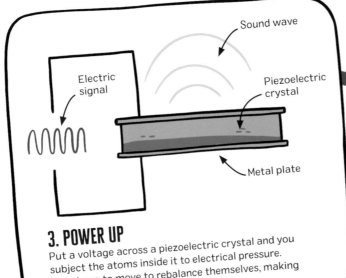

Sound wave

Electric signal

Piezoelectric crystal

Metal plate

3. POWER UP

Put a voltage across a piezoelectric crystal and you subject the atoms inside it to electrical pressure. They have to move to rebalance themselves, making them deform (slightly change shape).

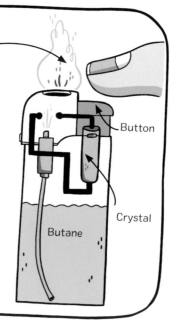

Pressure from thumb

4. PUTTING IT TO USE

Some lighters use a piezoelectric crystal. When you press the button on these lighters, the crystal deforms and creates the electric current. The wires connected to each crystal face produce an electric discharge, which ignites the gas. producing a candle-like flame.

Button

Crystal

Butane

USING PIEZOELECTRICITY

TOKYO SUBWAY

Piezoelectric energy can be harvested to convert people's steps into electricity. A subway in Tokyo, Japan uses the power of human footsteps to generate electricity for local lights and turnstiles.

SONAR

Sonar receivers use the piezoelectric effect to convert sound waves into an electrical voltage. An object's distance underwater can be easily calculated using the time between when the signal left and when it returned.

THE POWER OF DANCE

The world's first sustainable nightclub in Rotterdam, the Netherlands, uses electricity powered by the dance movements of its guests.

CHARGING ON THE MOVE

In the future, it could be possible to charge personal devices using piezoelectricity. Imagine being able to charge your phone as you walk!

ROAD POWER

Piezoelectric roads could make car travel more green by using the movement of car wheels on the road surface to power streetlights and signs. They would be even greener if all the cars were electric too!

SOLAR ARRAYS

Using photovoltaic cells to collect solar power has become so advanced that we can even generate electricity on cloudy days. But solar power is not a perfect solution to generating clean energy—large areas must be covered with panels to generate solar power. One potential solution that scientists and engineers have come up with is to build huge arrays of solar panels in the desert and at sea.

SOLAR POWER

The amount of solar power you collect depends on the number of photovoltaic panels you have. The best place to put these panels is where the Sun shines the most, such as in the desert. So engineers build huge solar farms in remote deserts. However, all the energy that is produced there must be sent to where people live.

SOLAR PANELS AT SEA

When we run out of space for solar panels, where could we put them? How about on the water! Placing solar panels on the ocean is not easy, however. The salt from the waves can cause problems for the panels, and some photovoltaic cells don't work well with too much sunshine. The biggest challenge of all is the movement of the water. In bad weather, floating solar panels would have to deal with a lot of movement—any structures would have to be built with tensegrity.

TENSEGRITY

Tensegrity is a word that comes from two other words: "tensional" and "integrity." Tensegrity describes how a structure can be designed to bend and flex in changing conditions.

PRINTING SOLAR PANELS

Engineers and scientists in Australia are working on printable solar panels. The idea is that solar inks will be printed onto rolls of plastic. The resulting panels would be cheap to produce, available in any size, and super flexible. This could be exciting for the future of solar power—think of all the unusual shapes we could print!

RECYCLING RADIO WAVES

Radio signals are a form of electromagnetic energy. We can't see them, but they are all around us, in the form of signals from cell phones, Wi-Fi, TV, radio, and Bluetooth. Some of these signals are put to good use, but many go to waste. So how can electromagnetic energy be converted back into electricity?

RECTENNAS

Rectennas were invented in 1964. They convert electromagnetic energy into electricity without using any wires. Rectennas are able to send and receive electricity over very long distances. They were originally developed to receive energy sent to Earth by solar-powered satellites.

SOLAR POWER FROM SPACE

Solar-powered satellites collect energy from the sunlight in space. This energy is then beamed down to Earth as microwaves. Huge rectenna arrays then convert these microwaves into electricity.

PAYMENT POWER

Contactless payment cards contain a small rectenna and a tiny electric circuit. When the card is brought close to an electronic reader unit, radio waves from the reader are received by the card. These radio waves give the tiny circuit inside the card energy. The internal circuit in the card uses that energy to transmit data back to the card reader.

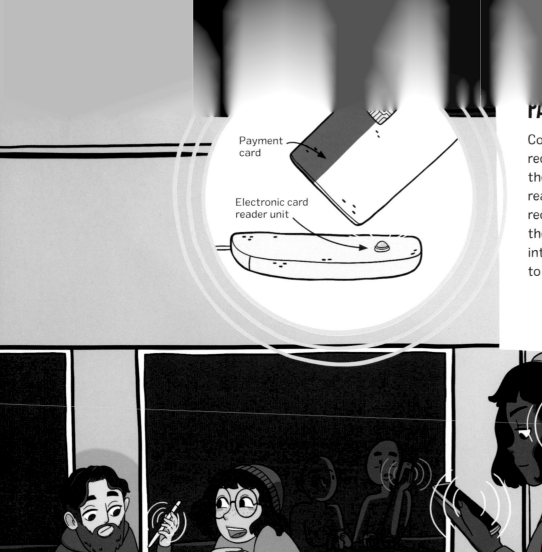

Payment card

Electronic card reader unit

IN THE FUTURE

One day we may be able to create electronics that use small rectennas to power themselves. Rectennas could also be used in smartphones to recycle unused radio waves. This would extend the battery life of our phones so that we wouldn't have to charge their batteries so often.

MAKE YOUR OWN ELECTROMAGNETS

TRY THIS AT HOME!

The magnets on your refrigerator are permanent magnets—they will always stick to your fridge. Electromagnets are different, because they can be switched on and off. This experiment adds electric charge to a nail to create a magnetic field around it.

YOU WILL NEED

- A piece of metal wire 20 in. (50 cm) long
- A long metal nail
- Tape
- A 9V battery
- A number of paper clips or pins, or aluminum foil that has been torn up into little pieces

INSTRUCTIONS

1. You will need to leave about 6 in. (15 cm) free at each end of the wire.

2. Leaving the ends free, start wrapping the center section of your wire around the nail. Try not to let the wire overlap.

3. Connect the ends of the wire to each end of the battery. You can use tape, but be careful because the battery might get hot.

4. You have made an electromagnet! Try using your battery-powered nail to pick up the paper clips, pins, or tiny pieces of foil.

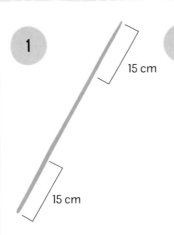

1 15 cm 15 cm

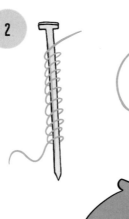

2

3

4

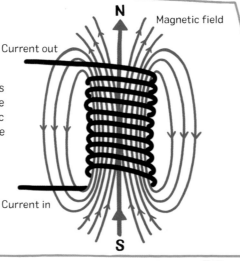

WHAT'S HAPPENING?

The electricity flowing through the wire affects the electrons around the nail, creating a magnetic field around it. When the current is turned off, the magnetic field will disappear.

N

Magnetic field

Current out

Current in

S

WHAT NEXT?

Experiment a little. What happens if you use a bigger or smaller battery, or a larger nail? What happens if you wrap the wire around the nail more or fewer times? What happens if you use a different metal wire?

STATIC ELECTRICITY

Static electricity is electricity that does not flow or move. It builds up when the electric charges on the surface of an object are out of balance. Here's one way to make static electricity.

TRY THIS AT HOME!

INSTRUCTIONS

1. Blow up the balloon and tie the end so the air can't escape.

2. Rub the balloon quickly back and forth on your hair or sweater, creating static electricity on the surface of the balloon.

3. Turn the faucet on. Make sure the water isn't flowing too fast—you need a medium-to-slow flow.

4. Hold the statically charged balloon close to the flow of water, then watch to see what happens.

WHAT'S HAPPENING?

By rubbing the balloon on your head or sweater, you are rubbing electrons off your hair or sweater and onto the balloon. As the balloon gains electrons, it becomes more statically charged. It can bend the water because the positively-charged protons in the water are attracted to the negatively-charged electrons on the balloon.

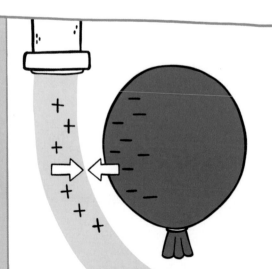

POWER OVER ATOMS

You can use your balloon to change the balance of positive and negative charges of atoms in other materials too. Try using it to pick up small pieces of confetti or aluminum foil. Does anything happen?

SPLITTING LIGHT

When light travels through a substance, it bends and is split into different colors. The shorter the wavelength, the more it bends. Red bends the least, so it appears on the top of the rainbow. Violet bends the most and ends up on the bottom. All the other colors of the rainbow appear between these two. Here are a few experiments you could try, to split light into rainbows for yourself.

TRY THIS AT HOME!

Red bends least

White light

Violet bends most

A JAR OF LIGHT

Fill a jar of water and place it somewhere the Sun will shine directly on it, such as in front of a window. Put a piece of paper on the side of the glass farthest from the Sun. The sunlight should travel through the water, then split out into a rainbow on the paper. If the Sun doesn't shine straight through your window, you might need to try again with a different one.

BE THE SUN

If you don't want to wait for the Sun, you could try using a flashlight. Place your glass of water near the edge of a table. Shine the flashlight through the glass and see if you can make a rainbow on the floor. You may need to try shining the flashlight at different angles.

COLOR WHEEL

White light is actually a mixture of all colors on the visible light spectrum. You can prove this for yourself by making a color wheel. Cut out a circle and split it into seven sections. Color the sections in the colors of the rainbow in order, as shown here. Stick a toothpick through the center of the wheel and spin. As the colors spin together, the color wheel will appear white.

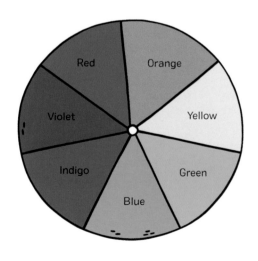

Red
Orange
Yellow
Green
Blue
Indigo
Violet

CONVECTION CURRENTS

Convection is the transfer of heat. It happens when there is a difference in the temperatures of fluids (gases and liquids). Warmer fluids rise and cooler fluids sink, which can create a movement called a convection current. This experiment will show you how it works.

TRY THIS AT HOME!

YOU WILL NEED

- Ice cubes containing blue food coloring—you will have to make these the day before
- Warm water from the faucet, with red food coloring in it.
- A large see-through bowl or tank of water

INSTRUCTIONS

1. Fill your tank or bowl with water. Then add the ice cubes on one side of it.

2. On the opposite side of the tank, pour in the red, warmer water.

3. Watch your tank to see what happens! The food coloring you have used will help you see the movement of the water.

WHAT'S HAPPENING?

The blue, colder water sinks and the red, warmer water rises. You have created your very own thermal-energy-powered convection current in the tank.

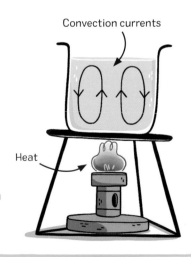

Convection currents

Heat

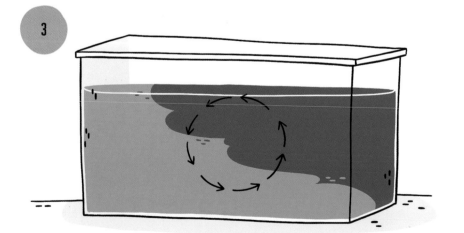

45

GLOSSARY

Atmosphere
A layer of gases surrounding a planet, held in place by gravity.

Atom
The smallest component of matter. Atoms are made up of protons, neutrons, and electrons and can be combined to form molecules.

Bluetooth
A way of sending and receiving data over short distances using radio waves.

Diagnose
To figure out what is making someone ill or what disease they have by doing tests.

Gravity
The force pulling objects down to the ground.

Mass
The amount of matter—or stuff—something is made of.

Molecule
The smallest possible unit of a chemical.

Particles
Small units of matter. Atoms, molecules, protons, neutrons, and electrons are examples of particles. On a larger scale, so are specks of powder or dust.

Patent
The right to use a particular invention. Inventors apply for patents so that they have the right to say the technology or idea of an invention belongs to them and decide who is allowed to make or sell it.

Photosynthesis
The process in plants, algae, and some bacteria that uses energy in sunlight to turn carbon dioxide and water into food (sugars) and oxygen. It converts the Sun's energy into chemical energy (the sugars).

React
Join together and change to become a different chemical altogether.

Satellite
An object that revolves around a larger object in space. Communications satellites orbit Earth, sending and receiving radio, telephone, TV, and computer data all around the world.

Shrapnel
Scraps of metal that scatter when a bomb or shell explodes.

Tornado
A storm in which winds form a column from a cloud down to the ground and can reach speeds of up to 300 mph (500 kmh).

Turbulence
Irregular currents in the atmosphere. Turbulence can be sudden and goes up and down and around, unlike ordinary wind, which flows horizontally.

Wi-Fi
A way of sending and receiving data using radio waves instead of wires. It stands for "wireless fidelity."

The Publisher would like to thank the following for permission to reproduce their material.
Top = t; Bottom = b; Center = c; Left = l; Right = r
12bl Miguel Sayago/Alamy Stock Photo, 12bc Evgenii Parilov/Alamy Stock Photo, 12br Asia/Alamy Stock Photo; 13br Shotshop Gmbh/Alamy Stock Photo; 22 ivansmuk/iStock Images; 34bl Ikuni/iStock Images,34cr Roksana Bashyrova/iStock Images, 34br Frizi/iStock Images; 35cl JohnnyGreig/iStock Images, 35b dottedhippo/iStock Images; 36 Roy Conchie/Alamy Stock Photo; 38 Franscio Javier Ramos Rosellon/Alamy Stock Photo; 39 GFC Collection/Alamy Stock Photo.

INDEX

absolute zero 22, 23
Amontons, Guillaume 23
atoms 8, 20, 26, 27, 36

batteries 7, 8, 9, 16, 29, 41, 42
Blanchard, Sophie 19

chemical potential energy 8
Clarke, Edith 29
conduction 20–21, 22
contactless payment cards 41
convection 18, 19, 22, 45
Curie, Marie 25

elastic potential energy 8
electrical energy 16, 20, 21, 28–29, 31, 32
electricity 4, 5, 7, 11, 12, 14, 15, 16, 20, 21, 26, 28, 29, 30, 35, 36–37, 40, 42, 43
electromagnetic energy 32–33, 40
electromagnetic spectrum 24–25
electromagnets 42
electrons 26, 28, 43
energy conversion 4, 5, 16
energy efficiency 30–31
energy transfer 16–17, 20, 22, 45

fiber optics 33
fossil fuels 12, 30, 35

gamma rays 25
geothermal energy 34–35
gravity 8
greenhouse effect 13
hot-air balloons 19

hydroelectricity 15

infrared 22, 24

Kelvin scale 22, 23
kinetic energy 6–7, 11, 14, 15, 16, 17, 18, 20, 23, 24, 28, 30

Lampe-Önnerud, Christina 9
light 10, 11, 13, 14, 15, 16, 24, 25, 31
light, splitting 25, 44
lightning 24, 28

microwaves 24, 33, 40
muscle power 10

nuclear energy 26–27
nuclear fission 26
nuclear fusion 26, 27

photosynthesis 5
photovoltaic cells 38, 39
piezoelectricity 36–37
potential (stored) energy 8, 12, 15, 29
power 10–11, 14, 15, 26, 30, 35, 37, 38, 40

radar 33
radiation 22–25, 26, 31
radio waves 24, 32, 33, 40–41
rainbows 25, 44
rectennas 40, 41
renewable energy 14–15
solar energy 5, 14, 15, 22, 38–39, 40
sonar 37

sound energy 16, 24, 32, 36
standby mode 30
static electricity 28, 43
steam power 11, 16, 26, 35
Sun 5, 12, 15, 22, 27, 38

telecommunications 32–33
Telkes, Maria 15
temperature 16, 17, 18, 20, 23
thermal energy (heat) 5, 11, 12, 13, 14, 15, 16, 17, 18, 20, 21, 22–23, 24, 26, 30, 31
Thomson, William (Lord Kelvin) 23
trees 13
turbulence 18

ultraviolet 25, 31

water energy 15
Watt, James 11
wind energy 7, 14, 18

X-rays 25

THE AUTHOR & ILLUSTRATOR

DR. SHINI SOMARA

Shini's background is in mechanical engineering, but she now works as a media broadcaster, podcaster, and writer, aiming to make science and technology available to everyone. Shini has reported on climate change, food, health, energy, and the physics of dark matter. She feels most comfortable when she's in the middle of an experiment or interacting with technology.

LUNA VALENTINE

Luna Valentine is a Polish children's book illustrator living in Sheffield, England. She's inspired by science, nature, and witchcraft, and loves creating fun, lively characters who often get up to no good in their respective stories. When Luna's not drawing, it's only because one of her three pet rabbits has run off with her pencil.